Back Home Awhile

John N. Miller

FUTURECYCLE PRESS

www.futurecycle.org

Published by FutureCycle Press
Lexington, Kentucky, USA

ISBN 978-1-938853-86-9

Contents

Acknowledgments

Habitations ll

Only a photo
freezes the house l first inhabited.
Snow, settled on its roof-slant, softens
its façade. What would be fresh white
in a present winter shows here
as a lighter gloss against the sepia,
its paint-sheen filmed in still driftings.

No one stands in front of or beside it.
Is this winter too cold for us children?
Are we inside? Not born yet? Father,
did you snap this picture
shivering perhaps, deciding
where it might be best to move?

Nothing shows except a structure
blurred by snow. There should be footprints,
father, leading somewhere out
of the Depression. Later
you should be trudging home from work,
your shadow cast by the lone porch light
shortening, absorbed into the past.

And mother, nothing of this white-framed house
reveals your touch inside,
your thrift offset by love of finery.
Haunted by absence, it's still
a typical Midwestern small-town house,
the first that you and father own,
set deep forever in its drifts of snow.

Homecoming

Too young to be my father's ghost—
in the glare of flat July streets
old men stop me,
seeking a past acquaintance in my features,
asking my family name.

Why this doubling
back to paternal haunts—
the stone-faced church, the vacant schoolyard,
the YMCA where my father worked
withdrawn behind an air of long, slow change?

The squat-roofed stores, the one good restaurant,
the shaded park and corner gas station
should be consigned to local histories.
Hadn't I left this north Ohio town
too soon for it to grow on me?

"Just passing through," I answer to a waitress.
The old men smile at memories and judgments
I can't guess,
recognizing something in my face
they give a name to, inescapable.

Just Off the Highway

When U.S. 30 ran straight through the heart
of Van Wert, I lay listening, inflamed
and itching as up-shifting semis
Bronx cheered me with flatulent exhausts,
regaining speed through north Ohio flatlands.

In a guest room I imagined Ann
also awake and restless in her bedroom—Ann,
my temptress. Fresh from the so-called
Paradise of the Pacific, I'd followed her
just off the road into a brambled gully

where fruit lay glistening and unforbidden,
clustered ripe in leaf-hugged fours and fives—
black thimbles bunched among their thorns.
Nimble-fingered, lips a purple simper,
she'd teased and tested me,

my tongue, lips, fingers stained dark red.
What did I know of poison ivy?
Hot as the devil's testicles, I itched
to get back at her. Outside,
trucks kept giving me the raspberries,

laboring through summer's muggy air
eastward on the road I'd take
two months later to begin,
I hoped, a higher education.

Stopping by Cornfields in the Heart-of-It-All State

It's hard teaching home-truths
to three smart-ass college boys, especially—
or even—if your name is Rose or Mindy
and you're a weary, over-the-hill waitress
lavish with your cherry lipstick
and honest-to-God friendliness that any
man or beast should know better
than to waste or put to shame.

But we're talking three hot-shots
who forget, or try hard to forget,
something as basic as their mothers' milk.
They've got you pegged, Mindy—your ample
name-tagged bosom drenched in sentiment
and yearning for a country music love.
Amid the cornfields of northwest Ohio
they park their seats of wisdom in your Crossroads

Country Diner, prepped for sport.
All three want apple pie with coffee, black.
One plays deaf-and-dumb. The other two
with nimble fingers forge his silent speech
you take for real as they convey, in words,
his order to your sympathy and questions.
Toying with their pie, they lead you on
and finally leave you with a two-bit tip.

Outside, it's high-fives for them
as they laugh themselves to tears
until the deaf-and-dumb one turns back
toward the diner door and sees you, Mindy,
staring at them with a look
he—let's admit it—I
prefer not to remember. All that ripe
Midwestern corn, and I there gulping spit.

At Black Hand Gorge

Lovers, as you stroll
arm in arm along the slate-green river,
think of your predecessors, other couples
on this same path or above
before they plummet from the rock-face
sheer in its drop to the Licking River's
sluicing through the gorge below.

Cling to each others' arms as evergreens
clench fissured root-holds and the grass
depends from meager soil. Imagine
jilted, earlier-day counterparts
nerving themselves for one last leap.
Listen: do opposing cliffs still hold
a long-descending, V-shaped scream
into the corrugated, walled-in flow?

Hand in hand among the strollers,
skateboarders and cyclists, move along
toward a serene stretch of the river
where a table-rock impedes its flow.
Ignore the underclothing, hushed and mounded,
mud-streaked, left there lying in the sun.
For how long? You can't know.
Keep walking. Nothing makes you go
in search of drowned or naked bodies.
The river curls beyond you, calm and deep.

The Quarry

Long ago, men drilled and blasted
into the earth for rough-hewn stone—
the monumental building blocks
of small-town banks and courthouses,
leaving an open wound in nature
rimmed by scarred, archaic rock
and later filled with jungle-green water,

in local lore as dangerous
as an entrance to the Underworld,
guarded by poison ivy, snakes,
and a rusted KEEP OUT sign.

The heat of adolescent summers
turns the quarry into a swimming hole.
Against parental warnings, in the shade
of second-growth Midwestern evergreens,
teenagers take their plunge, diving
as deep and long as lungs allow,
competing, self-assured, confronting death
by drowning,
                          grinning and gasping for new breath
when they break surface, as if born again
into the world of their re-entry.

They won't listen to the old folks
who claim to remember
a high-school football hero
showing off, who never came back up;

and tales of when the quarry, a raw gash
filled by little else but trash,
held coils of barbed wire, mattress springs,
wagon wheels—at bottom, anything
to snag a youngster worth
enough to render for the spoils of earth.

Near Dusk

the wind dead in low-fringing willows,
the river rumpled, mumbling along
its gravel-bedded flow, around a bend
a shape rears suddenly before me,
risen on its haunches from the shallows.

Heart thumping, I hold still
as it does, peering for its grizzled features,
waiting for some move, its coming down
on all fours, turning, lumbering
into the shelter of dark woods.

It outwaits me.
I stare harder, risk a closer step,
see a log wedged upright
in the river's gravel and, beyond,
a field with corn leaves catching

the last glow of evening's rising mist
where generations have unfurled the earth
in parallels, with horse-drawn plow,
then tractor, readying the land for seed
and autumn harvest—where I need

no bowie knife or rifle for defense,
the river smoothed to a mere murmur,
its waters void of great black bears last known
as carcasses in this part of the country
except here. In day's dying, golden light

for a few heartbeats an imposing shape
reared, resurrected from the past.

Baptism: Dillon Dam

A hush descends upon the sand-smudged children;
bathers link arms at the beach's edge,
a scene arising from my childhood—
a human chain in waist-deep water,
a man, white-clad, immersing them.

Where's the man? The white robe?
Who's being saved? my wife asks.

"A youngster, probably. That's how it was...
one by one held under, children
bathed in waters of eternal life,
elders singing."
                    Here, the lifeguard's
striding yellow-shirted down the sand,
lifted megaphone a magnet
drawing one more chain into the water,
drawing me from memory.

Already the two chains of bathers,
arms linked, move toward one another
in a dance devoted to salvation,
deep ends bobbing, heads high, toes
touching the lake-floor, wavering
then joining, waiting for their next command.

Should we join them? Sitting dry
and spellbound, I can't tell.

Who's being saved? my wife asks again.
We turn to see a man in white
leaving an ambulance,
rushing toward the lifeguard's stand.
The chains are broken; bathers crowd around him.
No child has risen from the water
dripping, cleansed of sin.

Heartland, Ohio

Trudging through thick, liquefied air,
you endure late August
swelter throbbing with the shrill, incessant
stridency of insects
                        near your road taken
slowly, its gravel glinting, bunched hot
underfoot. On either side
corn crops sag under their own weight,
draped stalks shimmering with heat.

Two half-crumpled beer cans
gleam in the grass at road's edge.
A township sign bleeds rust
from its bullet holes.
                        The insects
all at once go quiet. Breathless,
the land opens for you:
a rise of trees hazed by distance,

the road far ahead vanishing
into an obscure destination.
                        Stopped,
you strain to see and hear a pickup
revving, racing, raising dust enough
to trail it like a small tornado.

13

Biking Through Woods in Mid-Ohio

Whose woods these are we needn't know;
I'm thinking of our village, though,

where miles behind us lie its nominal
idyllic streets and housing tracts
such as *Beechwood Drive*
as we bike deeper into this grove
of the trees themselves and fail
to conjure its huge elephant-gray trunks
as bulwarks for some woodsy pastoral.

It's spring. Whatever it's called
everything should be in bloom
like Juliet's sweet-smelling rose.
Yet these old beeches,
gouged and splintered by the ice-load
of a late-March freeze, loom jaggedly
on both sides of our path.

What's in a name—the *Beechwood*
christening a street in our New England-
styled Ohio village, or borne
by clustered mammoths with their dates
and bark-carved pairs of letters?

This grove is ancient, dark and deep,
With names and history to keep

translated into German: *Buchenwald.*

The Missing Signature

"Mister, I don't sign nothin'
without my man, and he ain't here."
She bared her childish face, defiant,
sharp-eyed toward the world of strangers
I came from.

I tried to tell her that her name could mean
something for us all by helping
fill our petition,
my gaze dropping to her soiled print dress
and protruding belly.
                    "I don't know nothin'
about this sort of thing, and I don't want to,"
she said, wetting her lips, hunching her shoulders
as she stared at me.

I looked around, trying to keep up hope
against the ragged grass, the shack,
the tense hostility of hill people
transplanted into factory towns,
the trace of wistfulness on her squint face—trying
to garner one more name
lost already to an absent husband
and anonymous loan agencies.

"You and your smart-ass words," she said.

Heartland, Ohio II

The barn—what's left of it—heaves into view
first, half its rich-stained
corrugated roofing gone,
rough-hewn timber laid bare,
leaning with a weathered dignity

you won't grant
to the stripped-down, almost-stock car
flat on its axles in the field,
too old to run, not yet antique enough
to generate nostalgia

roused by the ancient Farmall, giant
rust-encrusted, armored tricycle
with iron bucket seat. You try to speed
past the blue and white house trailer,
the mongrel scratching at its door,

survivor too, you guess,
of run-down urban neighborhood—
its master, modern pioneer,
moving into old Ohio farmland
for another try

in which, it seems, so much depends
on a red plastic toy train
left under sagging clothesline,
a patch of beans and sweet corn,
a few chickens scratching near the barn.

Below the Panhandle Bike Path

near Granville, Ohio

"Gypsies," I tell my wife when we wheel past
the rising wood-smoke, unmistakable
odor of campfire, orange-crackled flame
from mud flats near a slow bend of the river.
I quote the first lines of a post-war
East German novel: "The gypsies have returned
to our small village."

"How do you know?" she says, needing
more proof than two beat-up vans
glimpsed through trees and underbrush.

We'd heard of cheeky little beggars
dancing, crowding an Ohio couple
in Madrid, fingers nimble
as the digits of two deaf-mutes
in dispute. When they disperse
a wallet's missing, and their laughter mocks
from a safe distance naïve Midwest tourists.

"Gypsies," the couple claimed. We've seen their wagons
camped on the fringe of trailer parks and junkyards,
half-nomadic outcasts I transpose
to scenes from *Carmen*
in their mountain hideaway.

"Get real," my wife says.
"Why must you fancy mud-flat poverty
as exotic, picturesque, and spiced
with mystery?"

"Call them *Rom* or *Sinti*," I say,
"if that's more real for you. Remember, though,
there's also poverty of the imagination—"
                              and stop short—

poverty of the imagination?
    odor of...
                unmistakable
                as I remember
a near-hidden corner
    of Freiburg's massive cemetery...
the huge crematorium
                    odor of smoke—
"The gypsies have returned to our small village....
Call them *Rom* or *Sinti*
if that's more real for you."

My German-born wife
stops her bike too, staring at me
puzzled   in a complicity of silence.

"Look," she finally says—
a fat man on our bike path, coming toward us,
dressed like a tramp, hugging two filled
grocery bags. He passes us,
reeking of wood-smoke, unmistakable
as the open campfire he approaches,
extinguished by each mid-November.

Survivors

Men in thick plaid shirts
and baseball caps, with wives
in scarves and wool slacks,
group around a trashcan's hobo fire
in a shelter ringed by mobile homes

for their golden years, perhaps recalling
childhoods when they sharpened sticks
for marshmallows, singing campfire songs.
Now they sit and smoke in quiet
or swap stories of the World War ll years,

settled in a patch of gnarled oak,
trailers burrowing in leaf-mold,
deeper month by month, as tires soften.
Bumper stickers from the Sun Belt fade
with hopes for beachside homes in Florida—

a far piece down the pike, they say,
eyes fixed on a wind-streaked pond,
autumnal leaves, and Flint Ridge Road
curved through wooded hills of mid-Ohio
toward a State Memorial.

Somewhere Off the Freeways

at Black Hand Gorge, or by some
gravel junction, we can still hear
trains dispersing their long loon-voweled
wail into the distance, mostly
in late afternoon, at suppertime
when few are near to witness.

We hadn't known those tracks rusting
out of sight in ever-narrowing
steel parallels still carried something.
We have no labor camps, have we,
no final destinations for our poor?

Could these trains transport
a few old tramps left over
from the Great Depression
or in their sealed boxcars hoard
long-exiled names that jounce and echo
out of nail-gouged lettering:
Nathan, Naomi, Jacob, Ruth?

But there's no profit in such baggage.
More likely they bring stone and brick
for the new robber-baron architecture
lording hillside farmland
gone to foreclosure, ironweed, and sumac.

Through Chickenville, past rural
trailer camps and the no-longer-mobile
homes immured in cinder block,
their metric click of wheels accelerates
a litany: *correct, correct, correct.*

Nocturne in Pale Blue

The slivered moon illumines little
of unlighted Brushy Fork Road
curving beyond my headlights' thrust

that lattices the white farmhouses
with moving light and shadow as it passes
rows of front-yard trees,

their leaf-bunched canopies compounding
the dark loneliness
of almost every house I drive by

except for those with a few windows
leaking the pale blue effluence
of TV screens

bathing the skulls of late-night viewers,
bark-flayed sycamores
flickering in will-o'-the-wisp light.

After Coming Home

A ceiling fan cuts
through the trapped air
where he's drawn the blinds, night and day,
against Ohio sunlight, passing cars,
and any country neighbors who might care
to look in on him.
                              Once, they say,
he trimmed the treeless slope of his front yard
smooth as a golf green. When the ironweed
and goldenrod grow window-high, his neighbor
takes a five-foot bush hog to them,
without a thank-you or a peek inside

where the fan throbs like a half-healed wound,
helicopter blades in slow motion
muted in the dusk brought home
from Vietnam. Twice rescued from the jungle,
in his white Midwestern farmhouse

he's ripped or hidden photographs
of ex-wife, grown sons, khaki-tailored self,
but he can't efface the images
of fellow pilots lost in combat.
He seeks peace in his gray exhaustion,
in being left alone

until the Meals on Wheels van spatters gravel
gunning up his driveway, or a nurse
keeps knocking with his medications,
or his neighbor's tractor roars,
hauling its bush hog on a weed-
destroying mission, helicopter-echoes
throbbing his darkness as the blades
stir sweltered air above him and his sweat
turns chill on back and forehead.

At the County Memorial Hospital

Through the panes of a revolving door
I see her sitting on the curb, knees raised
to chin-level, railroad worker's cap
shading her downturned face
as she draws deeply on a cigarette.
The grand hotel-styled lobby where I wait
is air-conditioned; even those
in wheelchairs and who walk by strapped
to oxygen tanks or with tubing taped
to forearm veins look fairly comfortable
while she's outside, self-exiled by her smoking
in the terrible heat and humidity
of early August. A loose peasant blouse,
bell-bottomed jeans, a pair of unlaced boots—
she wears the look
of an orphaned, middle-aging flower child
without long hair, wreathed in the defiance
or bravado of tobacco smoke,
sitting, waiting by the entrance
not for a friend to leave, not for a car
to stop and pick her up, but for another
cigarette before she stands,
approaches, pushes through the door
and nods to the receptionist.
Beneath her blue cap's sweatband
I see the character of her drawn face
as clearly as we read ONCOLOGY
above one of the corridors.
She says "Hello" to me
without expecting a reply
and walks alone toward the fluorescent hallway.

The Quality of Mercy

Only an abandoned tomcat
down from the country road
to scratch at your back kitchen window—
you see the raw wound near his underbelly
and relent, feeding him some watered-down
warm milk of human kindness.

He's one more homeless creature
lapping up all you give him,
rubbing against your ankles, suppliant.
Poor Tom's a-cold
or shivering with illness. You give in
and fix a bed for him, a cardboard box
with old towels to absorb his stench.

Poor naked wretch,
his life cheap, like so much existence
on this earth, *the thing itself*
you stroke in momentary pity,
feeling his bone-striated body
studded with ticks

and ask yourself if you could live with such
an abject flesh-and-blood dependent.
What are your means for long-term mercy?
You own a .22—
one fur-muffled shot,
a bullet through the heart?

Haven't you paid your dues
to Oxfam and World Wildlife Federation?
Why can't he just slink off in the dark,
grateful, and lay his misery
on someone else's doorstep?

Out on the Farm

A scythe, once on the cutting edge of mowing,
rusts in the tool shed. A red-painted pump,
long past its priming, forms a question mark
as to its use in the front yard.
Cows no longer come home
to the barn converted into stables;
white fencing is now *in* for thoroughbreds,
barbed wire out. Art Gentry, garbed
in boots and beaded leather, rides
his gelding with a holster for his cell phone
to call his wife and learn when supper's ready.
They have no dog to hound the deer
away from her petunias. Their lawn tractor
won't mow fields beyond the paddocks, rife
with *multiflora rosa,* sumac, ironweed
and blackberry. Their new ranch house, though,
is weatherproof, soundproof, and proof of status.
Their fireplace burns artificial logs.
From poolside they hear a red-headed
woodpecker tapping out a password
over and over in a leafless oak:
deadwood, deadwood, deadwood.

Before the Drought

A duet of quavered howls and snuffles
near the creek's still-brimming sheen—
two weepy-eyed hounds
parted the scrub brush, ribs protruding
through wet skin—one black with spots
of white-tipped hair, one white
with black spots, his lank partner's negative.
In a slack St. Vitus' dance,
pressing their hunger at our heels,
they dogged us toward the farmhouse.

No answer to our phone calls
to the owner listed on their tags;
no luck feeding them dried cat food—
the dark one gnashed and spilled its plate,
the light one rooted through our bean-patch
sniffing at our crop.

We lured them to the corn-crib, barred it
behind their rush for crusts of bread—
in fifteen minutes they'd slipped free.
We tried the barn with its new sliding door—
somehow they slid out free, howling
under our window, canine sirens
rising against our sleep.

By moonset, close to dawn, they disappeared—
the start of four weeks without rain.

Dog Days

Enough that late morning
hazes breathless where the shade melts
under our maple. Enough that
"Smoking may be dangerous to health"
as I inhale the pollen
thickening the air that feeds my lungs.
Enough said by the Surgeon General
without a word against the fungoid
sulfur-tinted clouds sprouting
in the rumbled distance.
Enough to bear in silence, if I could,
the full brutality of summer heat.
The air hangs dank enough without the newscasts—
flooding in the Midwest,
drought in California, forest fires
blazing, the war's latest casualties—
or our syrupy words to each other
trickling down my nerves like sweat.
Enough that afternoon will bring the rasp
of crows through clinging upper temperatures,
that evening leaves will gasp
at each small breath of air, that fireflies
will rise like embers from our smoky lawn.

Leaving Our Ohio Farm

What harvesting remains in winter?
Husks of memory. In January
the low sun must persevere
plowing just above a bleak horizon.
The days of this long month have shrunk with cold.
Time is a chain of frozen moments
and space the crusted acreage
impervious to harrowing wind.
                                   Should
we migrate south to fruitful Florida
where alligators graze on liquid warmth,
where sands gleam golden with false promise
never to run out on us
and, ah, where nubile girls stretched on the beach
ripen in sunlight, unaware
how gently, slowly they grow prune-skinned basking,
baking in their aromatic oils?

Into the New Millennium

Late March in February. What should be snow
pelting winter-rubbled roads
with rain and more rain pelting
raw, thawed earth made mud
by land developers. Late March in February,
drivers speeding up to pass
motorists on puddled, rubbled roads,
speeding up to keep pace
with the coming equinox, late March
rain on shoppers head-start shopping
for Easter after Valentine's Day
in mid-February, shoppers pelted early
by rain forecast for tomorrow, and tomorrow
road work starts one month early,
drivers pressing their accelerators
toward the green of traffic lights
installed last week where knots of traffic
snarl the string of shopping centers
opened early, spring
for Christmas bargains where last Easter
unfarmed fields held billboards
and for-sale signs. Late March in February.
Drivers press to do tomorrow's shopping
before tomorrow's road work,
pelted by an early April rain.

Not March, not February—
a raw, mud-puddled state in the Midwest,
drivers after shopping driving
straight home, spring around the corner
in their flower beds as Easter
crocuses force green tips
through rain-runneled February soil,
a weather-beaten neighbor

saying "slow down, we're still on winter time,"
with daylight scarce and rain-pelt sure
to freeze frost-rubbled roads again,
seeming to give the lie to global warming,
driving shoppers hub-cap deep in snow.

Licking Valley Tractor Sales

You think that you can go back
year after year into that low

ramshackle building
with grease-smoothed wood floors
and small boxes of machine parts
stacked or pigeonholed
and call in Larry, the grizzled,
heavyset old coot
who owns the place, to tell him what you need.

He always finds it right off, jots down
price plus tax, instructs you on its function.
You know he's a skilled mechanic—
a rebuilt Ford 9N tractor
sits outside, FOR SALE—
for years a fixture you know
never will be sold, especially
since Larry doesn't deal with plastic.
Either cash or check, fellah,

as he goes about his business
in his own gruff way—
no computer, no cash register—
the way he'll work forever,
you imagine, until
you look closely at his eyes,
their squinted, moist, far-off stare
of either pain or sadness, you don't know,
and realize

that you know nothing, nothing
of the death he's undergoing
or how long it might last.

Lightfall

At evening, when the blown
flakes of sunlight and its slanting
dazzle sink on the still pond,
a fisherman waits in the last glow
lighting his cast.

From the dam, he watches splashed
circles spread from fish hidden
under the slow healing of their water,
the closing of a sheen that gathers
coldness in the night air.

Now his bobber is a low-lit
outline where it drifts;
the sky's pallor,
glazed on upturned surface,
fades between the dark of mirrored trees.

Dusk thickens where shrubs edge
his stand, and insects chirr
above the ronk of frogs. He turns
homeward; the water slides its thin
silent coating down the dam.

No Funeral Oration

—at Denison University, Granville, Ohio

The box with father's burnt remains
sat in my closet, out of sight
for months, not wholly out of mind,
a carton of surprising weight

for such a shrunken corpse reduced
to ash. More an embarrassment
than reliquary, nothing sacred,
yet more than plain white cardboard bent

to hold a heap of furnace-dust,
it sat where I had hidden it,
addressed to me, the one child who
could best confer its remnant bits

on grounds I knew and father loved—
our alma mater. Should I strew
its contents proudly, openly
dispersing ash and bone in view

of faculty and students? Wait
for nighttime privacy and stealth?
I tried to visualize a blast
of heat, a man consumed, a self

candescent, ashen, all he was
in flesh turned grit-layer for those haunts
we'd both known—Beaver Field, the grass
where old Marsh Hall stood. Would he want

a witnessed ritual? My father
shelved in a box bestowed on me—
I finally crumble him in hand
and feed him to a spring night's breeze.

Acknowledgments

My thanks and acknowledgments to the following journals, which have published the poems listed with them:

Algonquin: "Heartland, Ohio ll"
Bellowing Ark: "Homecoming," "At the County Memorial Hospital"
Birmingham Poetry Review: "Licking Valley Tractor Sales,"
    "Somewhere Off the Freeways"
Carriage House Review: "Just Off the Highway"
College English: "Heartland, Ohio"
Debris: "Leaving Our Ohio Farm"
Epiphany: "After Coming Home"
Futures Trading Lit: "The Quarry"
The Heartlands Today: "Biking Through Woods in Mid-Ohio"
Main Street Rag: "Nocturne in Pale Blue," "Into the New Millennium"
The Orange Room Review: "The Missing Signature"
Pearl: "The Quality of Mercy"
Pinyon: "Dog Days"
The Pinyon Review: "At Black Hand Gorge," "Near Dusk"
Poem: "Survivors"
Pudding Magazine: "Habitations ll," "No Funeral Oration"
The Raintown Review: "Stopping by Cornfields in the Heart-of-It-
    All State"
Shenandoah: "Lightfall"
Tar River Poetry: "Before the Drought"
Third Wednesday: "Out on the Farm."

A mutilated version of "Baptism: Dillon Dam" appeared in *In and Out of Their Elements* (Waterbury CT: Fine Tooth Press, 2006), 27.

"After Coming Home" and "Lightfall" appeared also in my full-length collection *In Passing* (Montrose, CO: Pinyon Publishing, 2014).

Cover artwork, an artistic treatment of the original photo
"Farm Prairie Grass," by Brian Lary; cover and interior book design
by Diane Kistner; Philosopher text and titling

About FutureCycle Press

FutureCycle Press is dedicated to publishing lasting English-language poetry books, chapbooks, and anthologies in both print-on-demand and ebook formats. Founded in 2007 by long-time independent editor/publishers and partners Diane Kistner and Robert S. King, the press incorporated as a nonprofit in 2012. A number of our editors are distinguished poets and writers in their own right, and we have been actively involved in the small press movement going back to the early seventies.

The FutureCycle Poetry Book Prize and honorarium is awarded annually for the best full-length volume of poetry we publish in a calendar year. Introduced in 2013, our Good Works projects are anthologies devoted to issues of universal significance, with all pro-ceeds donated to a related worthy cause. Our Selected Poems series highlights contemporary poets with a substantial body of work to their credit; with this series we strive to resurrect work that has had limited distribution and is now out of print.

We are dedicated to giving all of the authors we publish the care their work deserves, making our catalog of titles the most diverse and distinguished it can be, and paying forward any earnings to fund more great books.

We've learned a few things about independent publishing over the years. We've also evolved a unique, resilient publishing model that allows us to focus mainly on vetting and preserving for posterity the most books of exceptional quality without becoming overwhelmed with bookkeeping and mailing, fundraising activities, or taxing editorial and production "bubbles." To find out more about what we are doing, come see us at www.futurecycle.org.

www.ingramcontent.com/pod-product-compliance
Lightning Source LLC
Chambersburg PA
CBHW060046050426
42448CB00012B/3129